Bush Theatre

MISTY

by Arinzé Kene

15 March–21 April 2018
Bush Theatre, London

MISTY

by Arinzé Kene

Team

Performer & Playwright	**Arinzé Kene**
Director	**Omar Elerian**
Designer	**Rajha Shakiry**
Musical Director/Musician	**Shiloh Coke**
Musical Director/Musician	**Adrian McLeod**
Little Girl	**Mya Napolean & Rene Powell**
Lighting Designer	**Jackie Shemesh**
Sound Designer	**Elena Peña**
Sound Associate	**Richard Bell**
Video Designer	**Daniel Denton**
Dramaturgs	**Stewart Pringle & Kirsty Housley**
Production Manager	**Michael Ager**
Company Stage Manager	**Rike Berg**
Assistant Stage Manager	**Hanne Schulpé**
Set Builder	**Ridiculous Solutions**

Arinzé Kene Performer & Playwright
Screen International UK Star of Tomorrow, actor and writer Arinzé Kene was raised in London to Nigerian parents. 2017 saw his new play, *good dog*, tour the UK with tiata fahodzi theatre company. His stage play *God's Property* ran at Soho Theatre in 2013, co-produced with Talawa. *Little Baby Jesus*, directed by Che Walker, ran in May 2011 at the Ovalhouse Theatre, where his play *Estate Walls* also ran in 2010. Arinzé was named Most Promising Playwright at the Off West End Theatre Awards for *Estate Walls* in 2011, which was also nominated for Best New Play. Arinzé was a part of the Soho Theatre Six group and the Writers' Super Group at the Royal Court Theatre. His original feature film, *Seekers*, is on the Brit List and is currently in development. Kene was involved in the development of the second series of Big Talk's *Youngers* for E4, in which he played the part of Ashley.

In terms of acting, he most recently starred in new E4/Netflix Original series *Crazyhead* and took the lead as 'Ade' in the Duncan Kenworthy (*Love Actually*, *Notting Hill*, *Four Weddings and a Funeral*) produced film *The Pass* opposite Russell Tovey. For this role he was nominated for Best Supporting Actor at the 2016 BIFA's and won the prestigious Best Supporting Actor award at the 2016 Evening Standard Film Awards. Kene has just been seen taking his talents to the London stage, starring as the lead in *One Night In Miami* at the Donmar Warehouse, playing soul singing legend 'Sam Cooke' and more recently in the hugely successful Old Vic Theatre production, based on the music of Bob Dylan – *Girl from the North Country*, which transferred to the West End for an extended run. Later this year he will be seen taking the lead role opposite Michaela Coel in Netflix's acquired feature film, *Been So Long*, and in a vital role in the BBC's new thriller, opposite Paddy Considine, *Informer*.

Omar Elerian Director
Omar is an award-winning Italian/Palestinian theatre director, deviser and performer, who trained at Jacques Lecoq International Theatre School in Paris. He joined the Bush in 2012 alongside Madani Younis and since then has been the resident Associate Director. He is in charge of the Bush's talent development, leading on the Associate Artists and Project 2036 schemes. He is also involved in the development and delivery of the Bush's artistic program and lead the programming of the RADAR festival between 2012 and 2015. His directing credits for the Bush include *NASSIM* by Nassim Soleimanpour, *One Cold Dark Night* by Nancy Harris and *Islands* by Caroline Horton. As Associate Director, he has worked alongside Madani Younis on the Bush's productions of *The Royale*, *Perseverance Drive* and *Chalet Lines*. Other credits include acclaimed site-specific production *The Mill – City of Dreams*, Olivier Award nominated *You're Not Like The Other Girls Chrissy*, *Testa di Rame* (Italy), *Les P'tites Grandes Choses* (France) and *L'Envers du Décor* (France).

Rajha Shakiry Designer
Rajha is a freelance theatre designer and maker, who works across the spectrum of scripted and devised theatre, dance, musical theatre, and opera. She was born in Iraq and educated in England, completing a degree in Mathematics before re-training in Theatre Design at Wimbledon School of Art (BA) and Royal Central School of Speech and Drama (MA, distinction). Rajha's work has most recently been exhibited at the V&A (*Make:Believe*, 2015) and as a finalist at World Stage Design 2013.

Recent projects include: *The Mountaintop* (Young Vic/JMK), *Mobile* (The Paper Birds), *The Head Wrap Diaries* (Uchenna Dance) and *Muhammad Ali & Me* (Mojisola Adebayo). Rajha's current collaborations include projects at the National Theatre, the Bush Theatre, and The Place.

Shiloh Coke Musical Director/Musician
Shiloh is an actress, singer, multi-instrumentalist and musical director. She trained on the actor musicianship course at Rose Bruford College and since graduating in 2014 has consistently worked performing, musically directing and teaching. *Misty* will be the fourth theatre production Shiloh has musically directed after having previously MD-ed the Donmar's Shakespeare Trilogy (*Julius Caesar*, *Henry IV* and *The Tempest*) for both stage and screen (including the New York transfer of *The Tempest*).

MD theatre and screen credits: *Julius Caesar*, *Henry IV*, *The Tempest* (Donmar Warehouse), *Julius Caesar*, *Henry IV*, *The Tempest* (Illumination & Donmar Warehouse).

Acting stage credits: *Into The Woods* (Stratford Circus), *Tomorrow's World* (Theatre Centre), *The Litter* (Bargehouse), *Henry IV* (Donmar Warehouse), *The Chaplain* (The Yard), *Henry IV* (St Ann's Warehouse NYC), *The Tempest*, *Julius Caesar*, *Henry IV* (Shakespeare Trilogy), *The Tempest* (St Ann's Warehouse NYC).

Acting screen credits: *Doctors* (BBC), *Julius Caesar* (Illumination & Donmar Warehouse).

Adrian McLeod Musical Director/Musician
Adrian is a highly skilled and experienced keyboardist, producer and musical director. He has worked with various artists such as Toddla T, Chronixx, Sway and Plan B. He has an extensive musical background that has developed his ability to be creative and attentive to detail. Adrian is thrilled to be involved in *Misty*, once again having worked on the RADAR sharing in 2015.

Mya Napolean Little Girl
Mya has always loved performing, and has attended Stagecoach Performing Arts (Barnet, London) since the age of 4. In addition to attending Stagecoach, she also studies ballet, jazz and acro dance at The Dance Studio Herts. Her love for performing means she regularly takes part in the masquerade parade at The Notting Hill Carnival, dance festivals with her dance school and stage shows with her drama school; more recently, she performed in *Dick Whittington* at Harpenden Public Halls – an experience she thoroughly enjoyed.

Jackie Shemesh Lighting Designer

Jackie is a designer of lighting and space. He works internationally in dance, theatre, music and with performance and visual artists. Most recently he has designed for projects as part of Manchester International Festival 2017 (Yael Bartana – *What if Women Ruled the World* and Phil Collins – *Ceremony*), for new work by Ben Duke for Rambert Dance Company and the Almeida's productions of Robert Icke's *Mary Stuart* and *Uncle Vanya* (both 2016).

Jackie has designed for many theatre productions in the UK including works for Lyric Hammersmith, Bristol Old Vic, Duchess Theatre and Trafalgar Studios West End, The Young Vic, Bush Theatre, Curve Theatre, Leicester and more. Jackie has designed the lighting for many dance companies including Batsheva Ensemble, Ballet Boyz, Arthur Pita/Sadler's Wells, National Dance Company Wales, Scottish Dance Theatre, CanDoCo, Protein and Avant Garde among others. Other collaborations around Europe include the Hamburg Symphony Orchestra, Steirischer Herbst Festival Austria and several productions for the Hebbel Theatre Berlin.

Jackie is a guest lecturer at London Contemporary Dance School and has given workshops at Sadler's Wells Summer University London, Tel Aviv University, The Place Theatre, The Academy of Media Arts in Cologne, and more.

Elena Peña Sound Designer

Elena designed the sound for *Hir* by Taylor Mac and *Islands* by Caroline Horton at the Bush Theatre. Other theatre credits include: *The Caretaker* (Bristol Old Vic/Royal & Derngate), *Pixel Dust* and *Wonder* (Edinburgh Festival), *The Bear/The Proposal*, *Flashes* (Young Vic), *The Lounge* (Soho – Offie nomination for Best Sound Design), *Boat* (Company Three/ Battersea Arts Centre), *Years of Sunlight* (Theatre503), *Sleepless* (Shoreditch Town Hall/Staatstheater Mainz), *I Call My Brothers* (Gate), *Patrias* (Sadler's Wells/Eif), *Thebes Land*, *Brimstone and Treacle* (Arcola), *The Christians* (Gate/Traverse), *Brainstorm* (ICT/ National Theatre), *The Kilburn Passion*, *Arabian Nights* (Tricycle), *Not Now Bernard* (Unicorn), *Pim & Theo* (Nie With Odsherred Teater, Denmark/Unicorn), *Mass Observation* (Almeida), *Village Social* (National Theatre Wales), *Quimeras* (Sadler's Wells/Eif), *The 13 Midnight Challenges of Angelus Diablo* (RSC), *Gambling* (Soho), *My Name Is Sue* (Soho/Bristol Old Vic), *Under Milk Wood* (Royal & Derngate).

Sound installation includes: *Have Your Circumstances Changed?* and *Yes These Eyes Are The Windows* (Artangel). Television/online includes: *Brainstorm Live* at Television Centre (BBC4 and iPlayer), *The Astro Science Challenge* (Online Television Episodes/Unlimited Theatre). Radio includes: *The Meet Cute* (Recordist/SD/Editor/Musician, BBC R4), *Twelve Years* (Recordist/SD/Editor, BBC R4).

Daniel Denton Video Designer

Daniel is a London based Video Designer and Animator and associate of video design collective Mesmer. A graduate of the University for the Creative Arts his background was originally in illustration and experimental film. He has gone on to animate and design visuals for a range of different media from theatre, opera, music, fashion, web and broadcast.

His original designs include: *Alice in Winterland* (Rose Theatre Kingston), *Flashdance: The Musical* (UK tour), *As You Like It* (Theatre by the Lake), *To Love Somebody* Melancholy (UK tour), *Ready or Not* (Arcola/UK tour), *Peter Pan* (Exeter Northcott), *Bumblescratch* (Adelphi), *Biedermann and the Arsonists* (Sadler's Wells).

Stewart Pringle Dramaturg
Stewart is the Associate Dramaturg at the Bush Theatre, working to identify and build relationships with new writers, commission new work and guide plays to the stage. Prior to joining the Bush in 2016, Stewart was the Artistic Director of the Old Red Lion Theatre in Islington for three years, winning the OffWestEnd Award for Best Artistic Director for his work in 2015. As a playwright, he won the 2017 Papatango New Writing Prize for *Trestle*, and his other works for the stage include *The Ghost Hunter* and *You Look Tasty!* His debut short-film, *Whisper*, won multiple awards across the world. He has also worked as a producer, KS2 drama teacher and a theatre critic for publications including *Time Out*, *The Stage* and *New Scientist*.

Kirsty Housley Dramaturg
Kirsty is a theatre director, writer and dramaturg and she is an associate of Complicité. Work with Complicité includes: *The Encounter* (UK/international tour – Co-Director), *Seen and Not Heard* (Southbank Centre), *A Pacifist's Guide to the War on Cancer* (National Theatre – Dramaturg) and *War and War* (Pleasance). Other recent directing includes: *The Believers Are But Brothers* (Ovalhouse, WYP and Northern Stage – Co-Director), *Wanted* (Chris Goode and Company/Transform Festival/WestYorkshire Playhouse), *Walking The Tightrope* (Offstage and Theatre Uncut), *All I Want* (Live Theatre, Leeds Libraries and Jackson's Lane) and *Mass* (Amy Mason/Bristol Old Vic/Camden People's Theatre). She is currently collaborating with Bryony Kimmings, Complicité, The Unicorn and the Bush Theatre. Her play *Myth* (written with Matt Hartley, from an original idea from Kirsty) opened at the RSC in spring 2017.

Thank Yous

Madani Younis, Ellen McDougall, Brian Walters, Alex Bort, Mikey J. Asante, Anoushka Lucas, Laura Castelli, Matthew Byam-Shaw, Fay Davies, Rob Drummer, Rikki Henry, Nina Patel-Grainger, Simon Perkins, Jessica Harwood, Miles James, Aleesha Fuller, Stage Sound Services, SLX and Bell Percussion.

Bush Theatre

THANK YOU

The Bush Theatre would like to thank all its supporters whose valuable contributions have helped us to create a platform for our future and to promote the highest quality new writing, develop the next generation of creative talent and lead innovative community engagement work.

If you are interested in finding out how to be involved, please visit **bushtheatre.co.uk/support-us** or email **development@bushtheatre.co.uk** or call **020 8743 3584.**

MISTY

Arinzé Kene

Preface

I've been told to write a Preface. So I guess I'll just launch right in and tell you how *Misty* came about.

I went to the Young Vic Theatre a few years back to see a play. I'm being ushered into the theatre and I get talking with the usher. He's a tall young wide-eyed baby-faced black guy. His name is Raymond (his name ain't actually Raymond, I've changed it to protect his identity). Raymond is fresh out of drama school, excitable, optimistic about the industry and full of young actor jizz. You know the stuff. He's energetically talking at me about acting stuff and so my mind was drifting until he goes, 'Oh I saw this good play recently... ah man I've forgotten the name of it... it's on upstairs at the Royal Court... it's a black play that's blah blah blah...' And he carries on describing the play but my mind goes off on a tangent and I'm thinking to myself... 'A *black* play?'

Now I'd heard this term used plenty before but that evening for some reason, it really landed and I said to Raymond, 'Raymond. A black play? What do you mean by "a black play"?'

'How do you mean?'

'I mean, *how* was the play black?'

'Well... it had black people in it.'

'Hmm. Right. Okay. Okay. Right okay. Okay. Right.'

Raymond tears my ticket, shows me my seat. I watch the play. I leave the theatre. Heading to Waterloo Station now, heading home, and I see Raymond, he's just finished his shift so we walk out together. He asks me what I thought of the play and I think for a moment then, I say fuck it...

'Yeah man, pretty standard white play.' I knew what I was doing.

Raymond's all like, 'Hold up. What do you mean "white play"?'

'Raymond, it had white people in it, it's a white play.'

'No-no, I've seen it... I wouldn't call it a white play... It wasn't about like... being white or whatever, it was a dysfunctional family, it was a family play.'

'Okay, okay right, right, okay, right. But Raymond. The play you were telling me about earlier, the one that you recommended to me, that's a black play right? It's about black people right?'

'No-no, that... that play was... it was about people-trafficking, it's a people-trafficking play.'

'THEN WHY CALL IT A BLACK PLAY, RAYMOND? If it was a people-trafficking play, why call it a black play?'

'Because... be... because...'

He looked out into space. His face fell apart. Then he said, 'I don't know.'

Then he fainted and I caught him just like in the movies. Nah not really, he didn't faint but he did go kind of pale. He got upset.

We were still on The Cut so I walked Raymond back to the theatre, sat him down and got him some water. He placed his head on the table. Said he was feeling dizzy but I know when a man is trying not to cry. About a minute went by in silence, he hadn't sipped his water. He really needed to process this whole black-play/white-play shit. He raises his head, his eyes squinted, he says something along the lines of, 'I don't know why I called it a black play, bro. I don't know anything any more. Just because there's mainly black people in it, it doesn't make it a black play. Why is it that in my head, the race of the characters in the play, or the person who wrote the play, comes before the actual play itself? As though that's what's most important about it.' He was shaking his head.

'It ain't just you, Raymond. We all do it. It's our mindset.'

'Fuck that mindset! Let's reset that mindset!'

The whole of the Young Vic Theatre bar look around to us.
Raymond was sacked from his front-of-house job the
following day.

After that night, Raymond was never the same again. He'd text
me nearly every day and stalk me into having coffees with him
where he'd chew my ear off about the whole black-play/white-
play thing. The baby-faced optimistic Raymond was now a
distant memory. He had become disillusioned. Making all of this
worse was that around that time everyone started using the D-
word again. 'Diversity.' It was everywhere. In the *Guardian*. *The
Stage*. *Evening Standard*. *Metro*. David Harewood commenting
on it… and Raymond would harass me over coffee like, 'I looked
the word up "Diversity", bro, the Oxford definition is "point of
difference", bro. A point of difference. Am I a point of
difference? When they say we need more diversity, do they mean
they need more points of difference? If I'm the point of
difference, what's the norm? Is white theatre the norm? Is white
theatre a thing? Are Adrian Lester and debbie tucker green points
of difference? Diversity yeah… this diversion to the norm, tell
me, who gets to say what's a diversion and what's ordinary? I
don't wanna be a diversion. I've been on buses that have been
diverted. That shit ain't fun. Pisses everyone off. It's long. And
maybe that's the reason why Suzman was pissed off, read this
paper here, bro, right here, theatre's veteran, Janet Suzman says,
"Theatre is a white invention." She says black heads don't go
theatre, her exact words, to quote her: "they don't bloody come."
If we don't bloody come then where did I meet you, bro? Am I
delusional? Let me know if I'm delusion, bro.' Delusional would
be a reach but he was definitely not okay any more.

A few months later Raymond and I are back at the Young Vic
again. We've just seen a play and I bump into a black actress
I know. We'll call her Donna. Donna tells me there's an
awesome play I should go see.

'What's the name of the play, Donna?' I ask.

Donna says, 'Oh man… it's the black play on at the blah blah blah…' Now beside me, I could feel Raymond begin to turn. He wasn't gonna let it slide. Raymond was 'woke' now. So the words 'black play' to him, meant, 'let us fight'… he responded like a shark to a drop of blood.

'Whoa whoa whoa. Black play?' he said.

'Yeah. Yeah, it's a black play and…' Donna continued.

'As opposed to – ?' asked Raymond.

'I'm sorry?'

'As opposed TO – ?'

'I… I don't get what you're asking me.'

'As opposed to it being a white play? Answer me!'

'No-no, just, well, it's a black play – '

'Why's it a black play? Like. Why though.'

'Because it is! It's a black play innit! Arinzé, who is this guy? The play was written by a black woman, there's black people in it, therefore – '

Now, Raymond leans in for the kill. I tried to stop him but I was too late. He says…

'Donna, are you an actress, or a black actress? Is *Hamlet* a play, or a white play?'

Donna was done. She could not answer, her mind was blown. She had to quit acting. Cos she didn't know whether casting directors wanted to see her as an actress or a black actress. Didn't know whether to greet them with a 'hello' or an 'eh-yo'. It messed with her so much that she was neither an actress, or a black actress, she'd become a shit actress. Never in the moment, never in the scene. Only ever thinking about her blackness.

Maybe Donna's made up. I don't know. She's real somewhere. Anyway. Whatever happened, it led me to write this thing.

For my sister,
Ndidiamaka Mokwe

Onstage

ARINZÉ
MUSICIANS

Also

VIRUS / BLOOD CELL
VOICEMAIL
RAYMOND
DONNA
PRODUCER
GIRL
DIMPLES
LUCAS
ASSISTANT STAGE MANAGER
AGENT'S ASSISTANT
AGENT

Track List

01. City Creature
02. Apparently
03. Locked Out
04. Uncle
05. *Knock Knock Knock (freestyle)*
06. Mutiny

Interval

07. *Reversal (freestyle)*
08. Sleep Paralysis
09. Chase
10. Geh-Geh
11. *Jungle Shit (freestyle)*

This text went to press before the end of rehearsals and so may differ slightly from the play as performed

ACT ONE

Scene One

Lights up. The VIRUS *goes to the mic.*

'City Creature'

VIRUS
A lot of crazy shit happens on the night bus,
One shouldn't settle disputes on the night bus,
Shouldn't settle disputes after ten at night, boss,
It's only ever gonna end up in a fight, truss.

Here is the city that we live in,
Notice that the city that we live in is alive,
Analyse our city and you'll find, that our city even has
bodily features,
Our city's organs function like any living creature,
Our city *is* a living creature,
A living breathing city creature broken in to boroughs,
Mostly living creatures are broken in to organs,
For the city creature each borough is an organ,
And if we're saying that the boroughs be the organs now,
You might liken the borough that I live in to the bowel,
So if boroughs be the organs of our city creature,
Then our motorways are the arteries of city creatures,
The high streets be arterioles of city creatures,
And each road is a capillary.

You'll notice that travelling down these blood vessels of our
living city creature,
Night buses are packed with blood cells, red and white,
Them's the passengers, you and you, it's a normal night,
Some of you alight, more of you get on and pack it tight,
But all is well,
Cos blood cell to blood cell there's nothing to fear,

Not unless something sneaks in through the back door before
the driver has a chance to shut it
And it's pushing
and it's nudging
and it's shoving up the place
and you can't see its face, cos it's got a
hoodie on its head
but *can* see its waist, cos it's got its
trousers down its legs,
so you can see its [boxer shorts].
[But of course],
you ain't judging,
cos it's nothing
that you ain't seen before.
You're just collectively 'aware' of him, and nothing's wrong
with that
cos he jumped in through the back,
and blood cells don't like scraggy surprises coming through the
back door in dark baggy disguises,
it peaks the nervousness, the whole blood temperature rises,
and for safety purposes, word to the wise, avert your eyes, and
sit in silence.
The doors close, the night bus pulls away, so now there's no
getting off,
And if you're wise enough! You'll know not all of us! Aboard
this bus! Are blood cells...
Nah,
One of us is virus.
Geh-geh.

Some toxic irreversible shits are bound to visit the night bus,
One shouldn't settle disputes on the night bus,
Shouldn't settle disputes after ten at night, boss,
You're only gonna get infected by some virus.

I jump the night bus,
And it's packed,
That's the only reason I came in through the back,
Cos when it's packed the driver won't open the front,
But I ain't gonna stand in the rain like a cunt

As soon as I'm on, I realise I'm the only virus one
Apart from the driver chauffeuring in the front,
But he's sat there in the glass cage
which implies that he's had his last days of virus rage
Anti-viral oppression probably rendered him depressed and
submissive
bereft of the spirit,
compliant, not a breath of defiance left in him
since they arrested him and disinfected him.

I'm on the lower deck,
The bus is so rammed, I have to stand, by the door,
I keep getting (*Nudge.*)
Nudged in the back by this (*Nudge.*)
Drunk prick and I swear (*Nudge.*)
He nudges me one more –
'Oi oi oi, watch it yeah. You see *me*? I'm standing here. I'm
already pissed off tonight so – ' (*Nudge.*)

I must look like a pussy,
Because this dickhead pushes me,
The whole bus goes silent,
How can I not get violent?

I look this blood cell in the eye like 'what's happening?'
I crack my knuckles, step to him and start cackling,
Other passengers back away fearfully nattering,
I get to happy slapping him, blood cell splattering,
Batter him, nothing else mattering,
Bet he won't ever, consider, doing that again.

Get off the bus,
Don't have to run,
I just *walk* away,
That's how it's done,
No need to panic,
Keep calm and carry on.

Scene Two

We hear a voicemail left by RAYMOND. ARINZÉ *listens to it.*

VOICEMAIL. Welcome to your EE voicemail.
To listen to your messages, press one –
(*Beep.*)
You have, one, new message,
left today, at,
6:47 a.m.

As our two MUSICIANS *become* RAYMOND *and* DONNA *and caption is projected above their heads reading:*

'Raymond, Arinzé's friend, thirty-three, chef.
Donna, Raymond's wife, thirty, school teacher, loves cycling.'

RAYMOND. Arinzé, hey dude, tis Raymond here.
Sorry I didn't stick around last night to give you feedback,
I had daddy duties –
(*Sound of the baby in his arms fretting, he shushes her.*)
She's been… difficult –

DONNA. Every time I change her diaper she does another shit!

RAYMOND. She's been driving Donna crazy, so forgive me for keeping this brief.
Bro, I hope you appreciate me telling you this as a friend,
I had issues, with your story –
(*The baby frets, as if responding to what he's said,* DONNA *shushes her.*)
I mean, the whole 'guy beats someone up on a night bus' thing?
It felt like another…

DONNA. Generic angry young black man!
(*The baby begins to cry a little.*)

As ARINZÉ *listens he produces a balloon. He blows it up.*

RAYMOND. I looked around and most of the audience were…
most of them don't look like us.

DONNA. They seemed to love it!

RAYMOND. As soon we walked out Donna turned to me and said 'Arinzé sold out and wrote an *urban* play.'

DONNA. Nah that's not what I said. I said 'Arinzé sold out and wrote a nigga play.' You wrote a nigga play so your work would get on. Ain't nothing but a modern minstrel show.

The baby begins full-out high-pitched crying, RAYMOND *can't shush her.*

RAYMOND. Arinzé, I gotta sort this child out, man.
Listen, bro, I'm sorry if this sounds harsh but… (*Pause.*) do not have kids, man.
You don't want none of this.
This will turn you into an angry young black man for real.

The message ends.

VOICEMAIL. To save message, press –
(*Beep.*)
Message, deleted.
To return the call, press –
(*Beep.*)

It rings. No answer. ARINZÉ *goes to the mic behind the gauze to leave a voicemail.*

You have reached the voicemail box, for,
'*Raymond*'
Please leave a message after the beep.
Once you have left your message,
key hash for more options.
(*Beep.*)

ARINZÉ. Raymond.
Donna.
Arinzé here.
Hope you guys are good.
Just got your fucking voicemail.
I don't know if you guys are aware but…
You're not writers.

Raymond, you're a chef.
Maybe you should stick to… fucking chefing?

VOICEMAIL.
(*Beep*.)
If you would like to re-record this message please press –
(*Beep*.)
Message deleted.
Please leave a message after the beep.
Once you have left your message,
key hash for more options.
(*Beep*.)

ARINZÉ (*after a beat*). Raymond! Donna!
I got your message… so lovely to hear from the three of you.
Donna is a joker, that whole 'nigga play' thing gave me pure
jokes.
I'm still laughing now. Was she joking?
I've never heard of that term before.
She *was* joking though right?
Because this ain't just some nigga play. My nigga characters
have well-thought-out nigga story arcs and shit. Haha…

As ARINZÉ *walks away from the mic his voice
(pre-recorded) continues to leave the rest of the message.*

(*Pre-recorded.*)… Haha! I'm playing, man.
Anyway broski… thanks for the advice, I'm gonna let it
marinate and uh…
We'll talk soon.
Beaucoup blessings,
Slugs and fishes, hugs and kisses, my bro.

ARINZÉ *has come from behind the gauze and is now
downstage. He takes in the balloon in his hand. He holds it
in front of him. He lets the balloon go. The air gushes out of
it. It flops around until it drops, deflated.*

Scene Three

The VIRUS *takes position near a large cube at the side of the stage. He uses the chair as a bike.*

'Apparently'

VIRUS
Later that night,
After the night bus fight,
I walked about...
And then... then...
I stole a bike!
And then I rode about,
I'm really good at bikes,
Wheelie,
I thought I'd ride and see the sights,
Wheelie,

A virus on the corner selling white,
Wheelie,
Lady of the night in fishnet tights,
Wheelie,
Red and blue anti-viral siren,
Wheelie,
I politely wave as I wheelie by them,
(*Middle finger up.*)
Wheelie,

I mean, it's one of them nights,
Not much to do,
So I call up Jade,
See what she's up to,
Jade's an old friend,
We don't speak much,
But every now and then,
She lets me beat it up,
I like Jade nuff,
Cos we don't discuss,
About 'How's life' and,
All of that stuff nah,

I text her 'are you able?'
She texts me 'come now'
I text 'ten minutes tops',
She lets me beat it up –

Jade's a virus from round the way
And even though she's proper safe, and proper sweet
It's only ever proper late, when we meet
You won't catch us broad day strolling down the street
Cos Jade's got a complic-ated history
And I don't want my name dragged into her misery
It's hard enough as it is out here on these streets
Let alone to be mixed up in some fuckery.

Jade was just a normal chick,
But apparently her mum and dad were crazy strict,
Apparently they wouldn't ever let her out the yard,
They'd crack the whip apparently and make her study hard,
Apparently that put Jade under nuff stress and with it,
The good girl, apparently began to rebel,
Apparently at school she started acting parasitic,
She bit a teacher apparently and got expelled.

Apparently there was a house party –
Apparently Jade drank too much and got wavery,
Jade started apparently acting unsavoury,
Apparently she was kinda fucked, like, proper fucked, like,
collapsed and shit.

Apparently when the party was over –
Apparently her friends tried to find her but they had to go cos,
Apparently, Jade was nowhere to be seen,
Apparently they searched every bedroom, toilet, mezzanine.

Apparently 'I don't know' that was the answer people gave
when they asked 'where's Jade?'
'Ptshh, I don't know',
Apparently, they tried calling her phone
Apparently, they assumed, Jade had already gone home.

Apparently while all of that was happening,
Apparently in the stairwell just under the scaffolding,

Apparently Jade was on the floor collapsed again,
Apparently when they found her they had to call an ambulance,
Cos apparently Jade was sat there in a pool of blood,
And there was something in that pool of blood apparently,
A little lump of something rolled up –
Apparently she kept saying 'get it away from me, I don't know
how it came from me.'

Apparently ambulance rode up and picked it up and didn't even
do much before they wrote it off and wrapped it up
And Jade apparently stood up and tried to walk it off like – say
nothing happened and so caught her up like 'hold up, you're
in shock'
and they wrapped her up, in a cloth, and took them both off and
rode off, apparently,
the sirens were turned off, cos there was no rush apparently,
vomit and guts on her dress,
it was all a bloody mess, apparently.

Reputations in the city creature, stay
Rumours in the city creature, don't go away,
Whispers haunt the place like ghost and people say,
'Jade had to be a ho,
What kind of girl don't know?'
She let them beat it up
She let them beat it up
There goes that virus Jade who lets them beat it up,
She's easy like that,
Derelict building fuck,
Splinters on her back,
Gave birth in a shack.'

I'm outside her house,
Dump the bike in the hedge,
I climb up to her window,
Where I sit on the ledge,
She comes to open it,
But goes 'shhh' before she lets me in,
Just so that I know that her dad is in.

I sit with her this night,
She massages my wrist,
It's aching from the bus fight,
I'm kind of liking this,
Cos no one touches me,
Not properly,
Most people cross the street,
Or watch me microscopically, but –

I hate it when she's nice,
I hate it when I come through the window and she's got me
a Lilt with a cup of ice,
I hate it when she tells me I ain't like them other breddas,
I hate it when she says the two of us should be together,
I hate it when we're hugging in the bed,
Cos I don't wanna put the wrong idea in her head,
So I go over to the window sill,
To smoke, but I can feel her staring at me still,
And she goes:
'Babe, I'm not being funny but,
Your hatred of blood cells hurts me as well,
I'm worried that if you don't mind your Ps and Qs,
Your mugshot will end up on the antiviral news.'

'Jade. Lissen. I'm gonna have to stop you there mate,
Cos you're chatting as if you're a saint, when you
blay-tantly ain't,
Plus, you're sounding like my mum,
Sticking up for the blood cells as if you wanta be one.

And I've already had her shit today,
Mum, of all people, saying that I've been acting strange
as of late,

She actually asked me "am *I* stable?" She blamed it on
the spliff –
She sat me at the table, she said she's worried stiff,
She said *I* act bizarre, she was all la-di-dah –
Steady chatting blah blah blah, said I'm being blasé blah
about it –

But "it's serious!"
"Not gonna watch you smoke your life away"
When she smokes nearly forty a day,
She raised her voice a bit,
Pounding her fist on shit –
I sit and let her grow her fit,
Chewing my ear to bits but then –
Then I try to leave the yard,
Before I fucking switch,
But here's what takes the piss,
Here this,
Mum,
She rummaged through my stuff,
And left it looking mash –
But as if that weren't enough,
When she found my stash,
She gave it all a flush,
She likes to keep it brash –
And bom, that's what set me off,
"The fact it ain't your ting to throw away,
I bought it with my JSA,
Respect? What you on about?
I never smoke it in the house,"
That's when I went upstairs to find her purse,
I reimburse myself for whatever she flushed was worth,
The whole time she's pulling me back, proper pulling shirt –
But I storm out, slam the door, stomp the earth…

And then I catch the bus to come see you,
And now I'm here it's nuffin but aggro you give me too,
So I'm gone, cos maybe I am going through some shit,
But I ain't gonna get criticise by some hypocrite.'

Me on the street again,
Bicycle seat again,
Wheelie-ing down the concrete again,
Wheelie!
The virus on the corner selling white is still there,
Wheelie!

The lady of the night in fishnet tights gives me the eye as
I wheelie by but I'm all right
Wheelie! –

A balloon has suddenly dropped down into the audience.
ARINZÉ sees it and stops performing. He gets audience
members to pass the balloon to him. They pass it down.

A beat as ARINZÉ inspects the balloon. Just as he goes to burst
it he's SNAPPED into –

Scene Four

– a meeting with PRODUCER. ARINZÉ *quickly hides the balloon behind him, under his shirt. He sits into the chair, which places him in the meeting with the* PRODUCER. *His back is to the audience but they can see his face because there's a camera pointed at him and his face is being projected onto the cube. The camera is slowly zooming into* ARINZÉ*'s face as the meeting gets more and more intense.*

[PRODUCER *is voiced by sound bites of Morgan Freeman from various movies.*]

PRODUCER. 'CONCENTRATE!'

ARINZÉ (*hiding balloon behind his back*). Sorry. I've been... getting distracted –

PRODUCER. 'Look at me boy!'

ARINZÉ (*hiding balloon*). I just, I keep getting these –

PRODUCER. 'Look at me dammit!'

ARINZÉ (*faces* PRODUCER, *he's on camera now*). Okay, I... I think I need a little bit more time to write this. It's taking a bit longer than I thought because... well...

PRODUCER. 'What have you been thinking about all this time?'

ARINZÉ. Well I... okay so, this is gonna sound weird. I have this friend, his name is Raymond. Him and his wife, Donna... they basically, they say I'm selling out by writing this and, well, ever since they... ever since they said that I've been getting these... you know what, forget it, it's just... the whole virus guy, getting violent and... I'm worried that the whole thing is lacking 'T̲h̲eatre' and it's too... 'F̲feat-uh' and uh...

PRODUCER. 'I like that story.'

ARINZÉ. Yeah, yeah okay. But what I'm getting at is... they called it a... and I hate using this word but... they called it a 'nigga play' and, I mean –

PRODUCER. 'It's just a bullshit word.'

ARINZÉ. It *is* bullshit but –

PRODUCER. 'To me it's just a made-up word.'

ARINZÉ. Yes but, the implications, it's extreme. To call it
a 'nigga play'.
It's really got me thinking now… are they… do they have
a point? Is that what this is? Is that what I'm really doing?

PRODUCER (*beat*). 'To tell you the truth… I don't give a shit.'

ARINZÉ. Uhm… it's just, this thing is gonna have my name on
it, and if people think I'm out here churning out nigga plays
and straight up defecating on my community, that's not a very
good look for me. They'll crucify me out here. So I give a shit.

PRODUCER. Do you?

ARINZÉ. Yeah it's, you know, the whole point of me talking
about this with you right now.

PRODUCER. 'You're quite sure about this are you?'

ARINZÉ. Well. I've been getting these…
(*Decides not to tell him about the balloon.*)
… I've been thinking about it a lot.

PRODUCER. 'That's cos you're a baby and you don't know
shit.'

ARINZÉ. See I didn't want you to get mad –

PRODUCER. 'You think I'm stupid, son?'

ARINZÉ. Stupid? No. You're an accomplished theatre
producer, well educated, I don't think you're stupid.

PRODUCER. 'Yes you do!'

ARINZÉ. I just… I mean, maybe sometimes you can be a little
insensitive –

PRODUCER. 'You question my judgement, my competence,
my intelligence!'

ARINZÉ. I… no, I trust your judgement, you produce such
incredible work, and I'm grateful for this opportunity, I just,

I don't want to be out here contributing to the whole 'nigga play' canon, if such a thing exists.

PRODUCER. 'You're no earthly good at all, unless you take this opportunity and do whatever you have to!'

PRODUCER *is gone. The meeting is over.*
ARINZÉ *takes the balloon out from under his shirt. A beat.*
Facing us, he bursts the balloon –
He's surprised to find that the balloon was filled with orange dust, and upon bursting it he finds himself covered in dust. Some of it in his mouth. He splutters.

Scene Five

The VIRUS *is locked out of his house. He knocks on the door.*
Nobody comes to answer.

'Locked Out'

VIRUS
Okay, this ain't funny no more,
Tracy I beg you tell Mum to open up the door,
My clothes by the bin though, you're taking man for joke,
If you let me in though, I'll maybe let this go,
At least come to the window, I know you're there you know,
I see the television glow, when I look through the post…
Like how can I win though, I'm on a slipping slope cos,
Everything I do's a sin though, man ain't sniffing coke,
Man ain't pimpin' ho's, man ain't dealing dope,
You see me hustling? See me stealing?
It's that new blood cell bloke of yours, it must be him, I'm
gonna kill him.

You pick him over me yeah?
You, him and Tracy – one big happy fucking family yeah?
Cool, that's fine with me yeah,
But tomorrow when the day's in,
If I don't see the rest of my stuff, you just watch, that's all I'm
saying.

And by the way, there's no keeping me away from Trace!
I raised that girl, just me,
She'll leave you too, you'll see,
When she's old enough,
And she knows enough,
Nah, you know what?
Man's fighting for custody – bom.

I'm the one helping her with her homework,
I'm the reason Tracy's been achieving,
I'm the one who's been to all of her assemblies,
You couldn't even show up to parents' evening –

ARINZÉ *hears knocking at the door which leads backstage.*
ARINZÉ *ignores it.*

'Uncle'

Seriously, what are uncles for?
If not to help you out when your parents can't no more.
I'll be quiet and I swear I won't take up much space,
I won't bring anyone over, I won't get in your face,
I'll sleep on the sofa, won't disrespect your place,
I'll keep it clean and kosher, I'll even wash my plates,
I'll even use a coaster for every drink I take,
And when I use the toaster I'll brush my crumbs away,
I know you like the poker and your friends come here to play,
Plus you're a Casanova, if you need me out? Just say,
I know we haven't spoke for – who's counting anyway,
I know I stole your phone but that was back in the day like,
That was two months ago, plus, may I elaborate,
It was a Motorola, let's not exaggerate,
But that is the shittest mobile, on the planet mate,
I swear down, I've grown up, and I'd appreciate,
If you'd accommodate, seriously wait, seriously.

Seriously, what are uncles good for?
Remember the time when you were late dropping me off
to football?
I missed the game. And what did I say? I forgave you Uncle,
Covered for you nuff times, you were my favourite Uncle,
But now it's *my* rough times I see you're changing Uncle,
I'm at your door, you're clocking me like I'm a stranger Uncle,
Want me to beg? Get on my knees? You wanna see me
crumble?
Is that it? Fuck this. You used to be more humble,
Yeah I'll admit that I'm a virus but you're proper fungal,
I got some shit on you Uncle, Imma give you a lungful,
I know you used to pick me up from school completely drunk,
You'd be swaying into other lanes and you'd mumble,
You'd overswerve and hit the curb, it happened more than once,
We'd get out, you'd faff about and then you'd take a stumble,
Think you're a saint or some shit? Think you're
a Buddhist monk?
I happen to know different, Imma give you a lungful,
I know you have genital herpes, Auntie told my mum,

I know that Auntie was banging that man at church Uncle,
I know you lost your job for laundering yet carried on –
Dressing up every day as if you were still going work, Uncle,
But there's a dodgy flat I used to go to buy my skunk,
I saw you hanging outside it, looking disgruntled,
I watch you go inside and after like hours gone,
I watch you stagger out, tie off, your shirt crumpled,
You walk the streets, sleeves rolled up, your eyes have sunk,
And every now and then you shudder, smile and grumble,
You slide down the wall and fall asleep in a slump,
That is until you are approached by a police constable,
They throw you in the meat wagon and I know what you done,
Cos shortly afterwards they raid the place and everyone,
Comes up with charges and somehow you get none,
Which means not only did you open your mouth, you sung,
If I were them I'd hold you down and I'd cut out your tongue,
I don't associate with snitches, don't know why I come,
You can keep your fucking sofa cos it smells like bum,
Think I actually need your help, think I need anyone?
I'm gone.

The knocking at the door persisted. Now the door bursts open.
Smoke and light pours out of the door, before a giant shadow is
cast across the stage, and walking out of the door is –

Scene Six

– a cute little GIRL, *about ten years old.*
She's holding a sheet of paper and a helium balloon.
She goes to a microphone. Adjusts it to her height. Puts on her
reading glasses.
Puts the sheet on a music stand and reads as if she's speaking
from a pulpit.

GIRL. From: sistakene@aol.com
   To: arinzé-kene@gmail.com
   Date: Thursday, February 10th, 9:48pm.
   Subject: Do not be the naked beggar!

Hey little bro,

Long time no speak.

All is good over here. I'm sat under the opepe tree as I write
this. I've just put the kids to bed, they're growing up so
quick. Small chickens are playing behind me.

I tried Skypeing you a few times to see if you could make it
out here for my fortieth! You didn't call me back so… I went
behind your back and phoned Dimples. She said you're okay
but you're stressing, busy writing. Mama and I are glad that
you have a writing job, but why didn't you tell us? Were you
embarrassed? She said you're writing a searing contemporary
urban gig theatre piece? Is that the kind of play I imagine it is?

Bro, I know that too much cross-examination can be
destabalising to a piece of art, so I'll just say this:

The GIRL *gives a nod to the band and they begin playing*
motivational music to underscore the little GIRL*'s speech.*

You better not be writing some red-hot buffoonery to pander
to the voyeuristic needs of the bourgeoisie.
Because unlike the past brutalities inflicted upon us, this
modern war is in the mind, working from a psychological
perspective.
This psychosocial engineering programme is disseminated to
you through news, education, radio, television, film –

deployed in all sectors right from the government to...
the *theatre*.

The GIRL *indicates to the band and they begin to crescendo
as she drives her point home.*

It engenders in our people feelings of self-doubt, self-hatred,
and when that's what you're feeling, you could totally make
up stories like, well, the one you seem to be writing right
now. Or even worse, you could be writing some gun-crime –
(*BEEP!*)

ARINZÉ *produces an orange water pistol.*

The type of story you're telling creates a national climate
that is insensitive to our plight. Thus fostering a consensual
national setting wherein which our people are more easily
mistreated and oppressed!
And this leads to our people being harassed and even killed
by the authorities for reaching for our keys! For reaching for
ID! Or for walking down a street to go buy a bag of Skittles!

*The music and her speech has hit the climax, she indicates
for the band to decrescendo. They do.*

I know you probably have producers breathing down your
neck telling you what to write but you must still retain
your integrity!
As Dad used to say:
'A dressed beggar can get fed, but a naked beggar cannot!'

...but what do I know? I'm not an artist. Why not get advice
from Dimples?

ARINZÉ *scoffs at this.*

I mean, she's doing so well. Her paintings are classy as ever.
And the collective that she's a part of, wow, I follow them on
Instagram, they look so cool.

ARINZÉ. Nah, they ain't cool man.

GIRL (*to* ARINZÉ). I know you don't think they are but they're
ahead of the curve, little bro.

ARINZÉ. It's all a façade. They're tasteless private-school kids, who come to East London, put on a pair of dirty jeans, say 'yeah deffo' and call themselves artists.

GIRL. You shouldn't be jealous of their success.

ARINZÉ. I'm not jealous, I just don't wanna be a part of some phoney collective.

GIRL. You should seek their advice.

ARINZÉ. They're glorified cultural tourists.

GIRL. But I know you hate asking for help. Maybe if you weren't so proud, you wouldn't be writing a nigga play –

ARINZÉ has had enough. He shoots her balloon with his water pistol. The balloon bursts.
It frightens the little GIRL and she begins to cry. ARINZÉ feels guilty.

The ASSISTANT STAGE MANAGER appears. She shakes her head at ARINZÉ as she ushers the little GIRL offstage.

ARINZÉ (*to* ASM).... I mean, you wouldn't get it, you wouldn't understand... I'm got getting advice from Dimples... anyone can sell a painting...

He begins to freestyle.

'Knock Knock Knock' (freestyle)

she sold a couple paintings and her ego inflated and...
...cos her work blew up, she got these new friends, and they're so successful,
they're so grown up cos they're pop-up shop owners,
their art work is critically exhibited, they're cool magazine contributors, designers and editors,
tastemakers with three thousand disciples and Twitter followers,
and their Instagram pics are so like 'nuhnhuhnhunhunhun you can't sit with us.'

Anyway, she's part of that collective, and they're like... so respected, cos they're like... so selective, and like,

part of me wants the play to do well just so the collective
could be like
'Dimples, wow, your boyfriend's so respected, his play is so
impressive, we want him in the collective.'
At which point, I'll be like 'Wow. Thank you, collective,
I mean, I'm flattered but, I'm not interested.'
Cos that would show Dimples that I don't need a seal of
approval from them or acceptance,
and Dimples would see that I'm a true artist and she's just
been pretentious
I mean, I was writing the other day, in the kitchen as I do,
And they made me feel like a dickhead for begging them to
keep it down in the living room.
I was like knock knock knock. Hi everyone, sorry to
interrupt. I'm Dimples' boyfriend.

DIMPLES. Yeah, everyone, this is my boyfriend.

ARINZÉ. Hi.

DIMPLES. What's up?

ARINZÉ. I know you lot are having a collective meeting and
    you're drinking – sounds like fun,
    but I'm in the next room, trying to get work done, and I can't
    hear myself thinking,
    so whichever one of you who keeps making that duck sound
    I would really appreciate if you stop making the duck sound
    cos it's so fuckin annoying
    Enjoy the rest of your evening.
    I'll just get back to my writing.
    Thanks for your cooperation. Goodnight then.

    ARINZÉ *goes to write. Moments later.* ARINZÉ *returns.*

    Knock knock knock – Hi everyone, I asked you to stop but
    you just carried on with the duck sounds, even more duck
    sounds than before,
    it's immature, and hard to ignore, why you laughing for?

DIMPLES. We'll keep it down, go back to your virus.

ARINZÉ. Dimples may I have a word, with you in private.

First of all, I think it's deep how you don't stand up for me in
front of company,
I'm a commissioned writer now and I deserve to be treated
more respectfully

DIMPLES. You are the one who was rude just now

ARINZÉ. How was I rude just now

DIMPLES. You burst in and said we were making duck sounds

ARINZÉ. You were making duck sounds

DIMPLES. No, that's just his laugh

ARINZÉ. Whose laugh?

DIMPLES. Redhead Eddie, Redhead Eddie laughs like that

ARINZÉ. Which one's Redhead Eddie?

DIMPLES. He's the redhead one, he lives downstairs now

ARINZÉ. Dreadlock Rasta lives downstairs

DIMPLES. Dreadlock Rasta moved out, Redhead Eddie's
moved in

ARINZÉ. Nah, you sure? Dreadlock Rasta loves it here, he
wouldn't leave these ends

DIMPLES. If you don't believe me you can ask him

ARINZÉ. Dreadlock Rasta wouldn't just up and go,
Dreadlock Rasta part of the cultural infrastructure – wouldn't
just up and go,
this is his home,
Dreadlock Rasta you know, you sure?
Dreadlock Rasta moved out?
Nah I'm pissed off now.

DIMPLES. What are you on about?

ARINZÉ. I'm on about the fact that Tony's laundrette is
a swanky coffee shop now
I'm on about Betty hairdresser's turning into a Bikram
yoga premises,

Plus isn't it weird that we're the only ones left in this
building who was originally here?
People like Dreadlock Rasta and Handyman Andy slowly
begin to disappear
I ain't got nothing 'gainst Redhead Eddie, but I'm not a fan
of how the Rasta man keeps getting replaced but the trust-
fund man,
it ain't fair… it ain't morally right.

DIMPLES. Wow, like, as if you have the right to discuss what's
morally right?
What you write ain't morally right.

ARINZÉ. Says who?

DIMPLES. Says me. Says the whole inner city, that you're
exploiting,
Calling us viruses,
Yeah that's very nice. Yeah that's morally right.

ARINZÉ (*beat*). I'm gonna go for a walk.

DIMPLES. Cool.

ARINZÉ. When I come back. I think we should talk.

DIMPLES. Cool.

Scene Seven

The VIRUS *is alone on the streets.*

'Mutiny'

VIRUS
The streets are mine again,
But it ain't like before,
Something's different –
The breeze don't feel nice any more,
Cos there's blood cells everywhere…
And their smell lingers in the air,
I ain't used to seeing so many of them round here…

That's a next ting,
When I'm by myself?
That's the only time I ever feel that I'm myself,
My self is weird man,
Need someone here –
Need Tracy in my ear man,
Yeah.

Everything about Trace, the way I love that girl,
She's the purest most adorest thing in this world,
She got a glittery soul, her heart's completely gold –
She deserves the things I was deprived of, tenfold,
Not even big things, the simple little things,
Things that's, normal, just normal like…
Things like, things like: listening,
Things like,
'Come here, sweetheart. Are you all right?
You're so kind. You're very bright.
Have I told you? You're the perfect height.
Thought I'd surprise you, look, that thing you like.
What do you want to be? What do you want to see?
You'll be that. You'll see that.'

Nah with me yeah? I had to beg for shit,
Either that or prove I absolutely needed it.

Just fucking… nuff basic things I felt to do,
Sounds silly but, I nuff wanted to go to the zoo,

And no one took me,
The time my year went at school,
Mum was tired after back-to-back night shifts and lost the
permission slip and when they tried to phone her,
They couldn't get through.

The VIRUS *recieves a phone call.*

Hello?
Tracy is that you?
Come this weekend, we're going to the zoo me and you
Why you sniffling?
Who's that in the background?
Why we whispering?
The antivirals? She let them in?
Yeah? They talking to her now?
What they talking 'bout?
They said I did what on the bus?
What proof they got?
How'd they know it was me?
CCTV – ?
You sure that's what they said?
He suffered what to the head?
It was a normal fight –
Who's that laughing in the back?
Oh... then why's she crying like that?
Yeah the zoo, you wanna go?
Deffo, don't tell Mum though, she can't come with us,
Yeah there'll be nuff candy floss,
Yo Trace, listen,
You're very bright. You're the perfect height,
And listen – Hello?

When a virus shakes up a blood cell, the organ doesn't cope
well, the city creature goes pale, the body's feveral,
Antivirals administered by hypodermic needle go on patrol, in
search of us virus people,
As they police through the blood vessels, we scatter like
roaches, we scuttle into the shadows like beetles,
They don't want us roaming in the city creature, they don't
want us multiplying, they don't want an upheaval,

A mutiny, cos they know I'm polyhedral and there's not much
they can do to me but lock me up and ask that I be peaceful,
They ask that you stay away from us, don't play with us and
never lay with us, they make you heedful,
They wanna eat my soul, they want us barefooted and broke,
they portray us as dark hearts and evils,
And it's deceitful cos they created us and now they hating us,
turn away from us, label us medieval,
We get angry and we shout and switch, they say we're
primitive, and that we're limited, uncongenial,
Yeah that's why it's deceitful, cos they created us and now they
hate us, turn around and put the onus on us,
now you wanna blame it on me? It's all my fault, the way that
I be? You're taking *no* responsibility?
Ah makes me wanna multiply and infect you so's you die, the
whole city creature,
makes me wanna rally all my viruses and start a massive riot,
start fires and pull off car tyres
and loot shops and the whole lot, and when the cops try to kettle
us we give them the heat like kettle pots,
give them that hot volcanic rock, raise our tops, pull out our
metal glocks, blow them out their socks,
gun shots like blop blop blop, the street cleaners are gonna need
bigger mops to soak what's coming up!

There's a persistent knocking at the door again.
ARINZÉ *acknowledges it but ignores it.*
The ASM *appears and rudely chucks him a wetsuit. She's still
disappointed in him for making the* GIRL *cry so she doesn't
help him put it on.*
ARINZÉ *talks to us directly.*

ARINZÉ (*as he puts on the suit*). Dimples and I had that talk…
she left me.
She basically left me because, to quote her,
I was writing was some 'urban safari jungle shit'.
Raymond, Donna, and some other friends, no longer wanted
to be associated with me.
They didn't exactly ostracise me but my opinion in the
Whatsapp no longer had gravitas?

ARINZÉ *gets a random audience member to help zip up the back of his wetsuit.*

And my sister?

ARINZÉ *now unlocks the backstage door. The little* GIRL *pushes in a shopping trolley full of water balloons.*
ARINZÉ *gets against the wall and braces himself and she begins to throw them at him.*
He tries to dodge. Some will miss him, some will hit him. But maybe he doesn't duck at all. Maybe he takes his punishment.

She kept sending emails – (*Dodges water balloon.*)

The two MUSICIANS *join in throwing water balloons at* ARINZÉ.

'Why would you tell this (*Dodges.*) depressing-as-fuck story, Arinzé?'
'Why would you (*Dodges.*) make this shit up, Arinzé?'
'What about your responsibility as a writer?'
'Don't you care about the impact it'll have on people?'
'When you reach official Uncle Tom status, is there like, a special handshake?'
'What about (*Dodges.*) people who actually live this shit life, Arinzé? Have you asked them how they feel about you telling this story?'
And I was like
(*They're all out of water balloons.*)
I was like, 'Well, it's funny you should ask that.'

ARINZÉ *dries his hands. He gets the Dictaphone. He presses play.*
We begin to hear ARINZÉ *interviewing a young man named* LUCAS.
On the recording there's background noise implying they're in some kind of communal space like a prison or a psychiatric ward:

… Okay so it's recording, just, test it for me, say something…

LUCAS. Wha'gwan, this is Lucas, mic check one two –

ARINZÉ. We're good just speak up a bit.

LUCAS. Cool, and I just talk?

ARINZÉ. Yeah just tell me like, everything that happened.

LUCAS. From where, from the beginning?

ARINZÉ. Yeah from the start.

LUCAS. Cool, well it started on the night bus then cos... I just
    jumped on the bus, through the back door, when it opened.
    And I'm there now, just standing there and there's a drunk
    guy, swaying, and like I said. I wasn't even trying to start
    anything but he couldn't stand straight, and it ain't my fault
    he can't stand straight, so I said to him... I just told him to
    watch it. He kinda fell on me again, so like, I switched, and
    we got in a fight. It was mad quick. The bus driver stopped
    the bus so I get off the bus. And... yeah...

ARINZÉ. When did you see Jade?

LUCAS. I saw Jade that night because, when I got off the bus,
    I was bopping past a corner shop and someone left their bike
    there outside it so I just jumped on the bike –

ARINZÉ. You stole it?

LUCAS. I *took* it. It was in my way when I was walking past it
    so I took it. Minor. Stealings different innit. I didn't go out of
    my way, it was literally on the pavement *in* my way. Anyway.
    I ride to Jade's now... Jade was still living round my sides
    them times so, when I got to Jade's, I see that her bedroom
    light was on, so I just put the bike in the hedge bit, I hid it in...
    the bush across the road, where there's a little park.
    Jade was...
    ... It's mad cos all the 'blood cells and viruses' stuff, it's just
    the way I see the world, I tried to like, tell Jade about it...
    she said I was tweaking out haha said I was buggin out cos
    of some bad weed so we argued about that for a bit... I just
    see things differently, the whole blood cells verses virus
    thing is like, I don't think it's down to anything I was
    smoking... anyway things escalated and I left Jade's...

ARINZÉ. Where'd you go?

LUCAS. Went home. Rode home. Clocked that Mum had locked me out. It wasn't the first time but like… I knew it was serious because all my stuff was in bin bags outside. Proper raw. Ike, I didn't even do nothing to deserve it this time…

While the recording plays, ARINZÉ *leaves the stage.*
He returns with an air blower and a huge balloon.
He begins to inflate the balloon with the blower. It gets
bigger and bigger until it explodes with a massive BANG!

Lights out is simultaneous with the loud bang.

End of Act One.

Interval.

ACT TWO

Scene One

When the audience re-enter the theatre there is a balloon centerstage, six foot in diameter. Our MUSICIANS *go behind the gauze and become* RAYMOND *and* DONNA.

VOICEMAIL.
  (*Beep.*)
  You have, one, new message,
  left today, at,
  2:04, a.m.
  From, Raymond,
  And, Donna,
  And, the baby.

RAYMOND.... and okay, it's a true story, but like, so what.
  It doesn't matter that it's a true story. It doesn't make it okay
  to tell a story, cos it's true. What I'm saying is that you're
  falling into the trap that some of our black writers fall into.
  It seems that some black writers 'conveniently' wanna write
  narratives that majority white audiences are interested in
  seeing about black people.

DONNA. 'Conveniently.'

RAYMOND. And that narrative my brother, is –

DONNA. Black trauma.

RAYMOND. I would've just said 'trauma'.

DONNA. Black trauma ought to be a genre of its own cos under
  the umbrella of black trauma comes your typical stories of
  racism, slavery, crime and violence you know...

RAYMOND.... drugs, gangs, poverty.

DONNA. *Django*? *Django Un*-fuckin-*chained*. Give me
strength. Why do you think *Django* and *12 Years a Slave* are
always gonna be box-office hits?
Meanwhile something like *Love Jones* or *Brown Sugar*,
where the black folk are just going through normal
mundane things,
like being unlucky in love, those stories don't do well,
know why?
Cos the black folk in those stories ain't suffering.
We never get a cycling-through-the-city montage in films.
I want a cycling-through-the-city montage of a girl who
looks like me.
Cos I love a cycle. I really like cycling.

RAYMOND. And I ain't saying you've written *Django* but,
you've written just another hood story.
(*Their daughter frets.*)
Do you really want for our daughter to see yet another one?

DONNA. Is that the only story about us that there is to tell her?

RAYMOND. I don't believe that your story being true excuses it.

DONNA. But, you know, put your little nigga play on sweetie,
haha,
You do what you gotta do and we'll do what we gotta do.

RAYMOND. Donna, don't say that –

DONNA. No, don't censor me, I mean it.
If we can shut down some Barbican-arts-centre-human-zoo-
slavery bullshit,
then we can set fire to a little bush –
(*The baby is crying now.*)

RAYMOND. She's joking man.

DONNA. Joking as ever but I'm serious as fuck though.

The voicemail ends.

VOICEMAIL. To save –
(*Beep.*)

Message, deleted.
To return the –
(*Beep*.)

It rings once then goes to voicemail.
A light slowly comes up on the balloon and we realise that
ARINZÉ *is inside it. He's on his phone, leaving a message.*

You have reached the voicemail box, for,
'*Raymond*'
Please leave a message after the beep.
Once you have left your message,
key hash for more options.
(*Beep*.)

ARINZÉ. Hey, Raymond, Donna. Arinzé here. Erm.
Sorry if it sounds a bit echoey, I'm just…
Listen, I don't think you can dismiss Lucas's story on
account of…
it being depressing as fuck.
I grew up with him and,
he'd never been to see any of my work and when I asked
why…
Well… you know what he said would make him come to
the theatre?
He wanted to see himself there. That's what he said. He
wanted to see himself.
So me putting him on stage so he could see himself, is that
so bad? Am I fucked up, for doing that? Doesn't his story
deserve to be told too?
I mean, he's been through so much in his life and… given
what's happened with him since I started writing the play…
It's felt like my duty or that I owe it him to…

ARINZÉ *repositions himself in the balloon. He continues*
talking while he does. Eventually he's upside down, half in
and half out of the balloon, his back facing the audience
while balancing on his shoulders. His hands are gesturing as
he's speaking. It's absurd.

Know what, if anything, going back to the recording made
me wanna tell the story even more because,

I realised that I heard it wrong. The whole blood cells and
viruses thing, I had it wrong.
Lucas was saying that *he* was the blood cell and *they* were
the viruses.
Which makes more sense now because… scientifically…
If viruses invade the body, and raid the body, then Lucas and
I have witnessed viruses invade our area.
It started with them building the overground train…

ARINZÉ *starts freestyling. The* MUSICIANS *join in when
they pick up his rhythm.*

'Reversal' (freestyle)

– and because of this overground train the viruses came,
from far and wide.
Viruses raise the rent price so high that small businesses,
local businesses
that have been here a long time, can no longer survive
so they close down, so the viruses turn it into a Starbucks now,
which causes the property value to rise even more,
buildings are privatised even more,
which attracts even more virus vultures
pushes out even more business owners,
and we lose even more of our culture,
and even more people who used to live here can't afford to,
people like me, Lu, and Dreadlock Rasta too, that's what
viruses do.
So I had it the wrong way round. We're the blood cells.
We've been the blood cells all along
A virus can't replicate itself all alone, it must infect a cell
They inject themselves into a cell and convert that cell into
a mindless virus-producing cell –
It's what Redhead Eddie did to my girl –
And it was happening in the story as well.

ARINZÉ *pulls himself out of the balloon. He's still wearing
his wetsuit.*

Scene Two

ARINZÉ *doesn't seem to be able to move.*
As he performs this song, the ASM *gets him out of the wetsuit*
and dresses him.

'Sleep Paralysis'

BLOOD CELL
The sun rises,
My brain's awake,
My body ain't,
Sleep paralysis,
I'm always having this,
I can breathe,
But fear that any moment someone's coming to suffocate me,
Which makes me anxious,
Which makes my heart race,
All they need to do is hold a pillow on my face,
Or pull a plastic bag over my head,
Or pinch my nose,
Can't even fucking wiggle my toes.

I hear people walking,
With their hard shoes,
On their ways to work,
In my area, no one used to wear hard shoes to work,
But my area's been changing,
They've been replacing, us blood cells with more viruses,
Viruses who wear suits to work,
And hard shoes to work,
And us blood cells, who they say don't choose to work –
Who they say refuse to work,
Have to leave our places as the rent inflates beyond our wages.

I hear drilling,
Builders shouting,
Employed by new viruses –
Fitting extensions on their houses,
I hear women,
Here come yummy mummies and French au pairs,

Pushing wide-as-fuck prams everywhere,
Now there's ramps, where there used to be stairs,
Soon there's gonna be a separate lane for prams,
Cos they're the single leading cause of pavement traffic jams,
It's pramageddon,
This is my nightmare, I need to wake up!

They've even built coffee shops where they used to sell beers –
Where arty viruses meet up and chew off each other's ears,
And further down the road, they've built a theatre,
But us blood cells don't watch bearded men in leotards,
Thank you very much but fuck Shakespeare,
This is where I grew up,
The other day I was on the bus, and I missed my stop,
I did not recognise it,
Cos these viruses have come here and gentrified it,
And to be fair it does looks nice, but I don't like it.

Scene Three

'Chase'

BLOOD CELL
'Now, I know you hate it when I visit while you're working,
Jade,
I know you've got all these viruses to be serving, Jade –
And, I would've texted you, but my battery's done –
Which is probably for the best cos, if I switch it on…
Huh, don't even wanna say with all these viruses watching –
Come we step outside a sec, gotta tell you something,
I did not come all this way to be ignored,
Don't make me have to switch, why you acting silly for?
Telling customers you've never seen me before,
Like last night we weren't mashing on your bedroom floor,
You gonna blank me yeah? Pretend like I'm not here?
You think I won't start flipping tables and dashing chairs?'

She goes and gets a next waiter to cover,
She pushes me through the kitchen and out the back door –
Screaming in my face, says I'll get her in trouble –
She's up for a promotion and why am I trying to get her
sacked for.

She knows that there's a warrant out for my arrest,
Knows I'm already front page of the *Daily Gazette*,
Apparently it's quickly circulating via text,
Apparently her dad texted her, 'have you seen it yet?'
Apparently her dad got five brothers,
Apparently he's got a couple nasty cousins,
Apparently they wanna catch me before the police,
Apparently man ain't safe any more on these streets,
Apparently a normal person would be scared –
Apparently the fact I'm smiling and don't care is kind of weird,
to her,
Jade says my time is up, and she should be working,
She thinks I'll let her storm off without getting a word in.

I grab her arm and say –
'I won't let go unless you promise to meet me later with food
money and clothes.'

She pulls away from me and
She storms off without saying yes or no but I know she's
gonna show.

When I go –
I walk with my head low, and stay away from main roads, cos
they're the arterioles.
And when I'm passing people on the pavement
I cover my face a bit, pretending I'm speaking on the phone.
When I hear sirens
I'm diving, hiding, in phone boxes, behind a bin, behind a skip.
That's where I see
Kids bunking off of school so I tax each of them, for enough to
buy fish and chips.
I eat it facing the wall
Down a cul-de-sac, looking over my back, I've never been
hungry like this.

I feel like an animal
Scoffing it down so quick, the salt and vinegar's stinging
off my lips.
I have a bit of change
So I get a drink, from the corner shop, a can of Lilt, I finish it,
in two sips.
I arrive at the gates
of Tracy's school, for three-thirty, just in time, to hear the pips.
I decide to wait
Across the street, disguised by this random hat, that I found,
laying on the ground.
The kids pour out of the school
And my eyes are peeled for Tracy, because she don't hang
around.

I spot my little sister
Power-walking through the crowd, but she looks upset, got her
head down.
A couple kids
Trying to bully her, but I can't make out what they're saying,
over all the sound.
I'm tempted to fuck them up
But I don't wanna blow my cover, so I just watch it carry on.

And turns out she didn't need me anyway
She smacks the bully in his face and sends him crying to
his mum
I walk over to her
And I whisper in her ear, telling her when to meet me and
where.
But then some kids
Start shouting 'it's him, it's him', then the antiviral appear.

I run like a dog
Run like an animal, run like a beast, through alleyways
and streets.
Run till I can't feel my feet
But I still hear police dogs, barking, they're closing in on me.
The dogs can smell me easily
Cos I'm sweating, from the running, and I ain't had a shower.
So I tek off all my clothes
I dump them in the bushes, and then I jump in the canal.

When I was young
I never got my certificate for swimming ten metres cos I can't
fucking swim.
I dove in this canal on a whim
Hoping that after a few bad strokes my *instincts* would kick in.
They *don't* kick in
I breathe in water, I'm guzzling nuff water, I'm drowning
in the water.

I'm really trying
To be breast-stroking in the water, but all's I'm doing is choking
in the water.
I come to terms
With the fact that I'm gonna die so I stop panicking and let
myself go.
That's when I feel
Something under my toes and come to realise, yep this canal's
quite shallow.

I wade through the water
I get out, I tiptoe to a park, and hide behind trees.
I'm butt naked

It's really windy, and now my nose is blocked, cos it's zero
degrees.
So when I spot a hipster
Walking through the park, I rob his clothes, he's about my same
build and height
I put it on but
Something's wrong cos, somehow, it ends up proper tight.
I cannot walk in these jeans
I can't even bend my knees, I can see every muscle in my thigh.
But my area's been gentrified
So dressing like an arty virus, is not a bad disguise.
I stop, to see the clock
Through the window, of a shop, and remember that I got to
meet Jade.
But with no means to tell her
I'll be late, cos I lost my phone, when I dashed my clothes, in
the escapade.

I run
With a wedgie chafing in my bum, down arterioles, and I'm
wearing *hard* shoes.
People still look at me
But now it's differently, not suspiciously, like what I'm used to.
I get to
The corner of the road, where I told Jade to go, but I don't see
Jade there.
But I know
She was here recently, the smell of her Blue Freeze hair gel,
lingers in the air.
Do I go left
Go right, straight ahead, or do I just wait here instead?
The longer I contemplate
is the further that she's possibly walking away, but I know
Jade's head.
I wait five minutes
Then Jade approaches, slurping a can of Coke, and 'I know who
the Lilt's for.'
I locate an open car
I put Jade in the back, get in after, and I shut the door.

It's been a tough long day
It's been such a rough day, my stress levels have been
gone crazy.
It feels good
To just sit down a sec, to catch my breath and decompress with
Jade but.
I get vex when she
Hands me only ten pounds, and explains 'that's all the money
I can spare.'
I get vex when she goes
'I can't steal my dad's clothes, he would notice, there's nothing
he don't wear.'

I get vex at
'why would I lie, if there was leftovers at the restaurant
I would've brung it.'
I get vex cos
Up to now she's been all over me and now she's acting like she
ain't on it.
Nonetheless
I try warn her regardless about the viruses taking over the city
creature.
She says I'm crazy
Says I need to see someone, she says bye, and she's gone.

It's like I'm the only one who can see what's going on.
Call it virus invasion,
Call it gentrification,
Call whatever you want,
It's nothing but modern-day colonisation.

We gotta wake the fuck up outta this nightmare,
I've had enough of being powerless, enough sleep paralysis,
Can't you see what's going on, we're being ousted,
By these shiny-shoe-wearing viruses,

They up the rent and kick out the blood cell tenants,
They shutting down the youth clubs and youth centres,
To build a bar & grill with a garden terrace,
There's enough to impel us to desperate *measures*,

Let us wake up out of our night *terrors*,
Let us stand united 'gainst the *oppressors*,
Let us activate and organise *vengeance*,
Let us bring back our small *businesses*,

Let us kick them out of our *premises*,
Then let us gather all of these *aggressors*,
And make *them reside,* in death-trap *housing*,
See how *they* like all the heat, and *howling*,

There's gonna be black smoke *rising again*,
Cos my people are done *internalising again,*
Cos we don't wanna hear *apologising* again,
It's time to start *Penalizing!*

To high heaven we've been *compromising,*
But they're down with Lucifer *harmonising,*
That's why no justice is *materialising,*
It's time we start *chastising!*

A member of the audience's phone begins to ring.
This makes ARINZÉ *break character and stop performing.*

ARINZÉ (*to audience*). You gonna switch it off?
  Is that you?

Eventually, ARINZÉ *realises the ringing is his personal*
phone that he left somewhere on stage. He's very
apologetic…

Ah shit, my bad…
I was texting at the interval and…

He turns the ringer off but it's vibrating in his hand.
ARINZÉ *looks at the caller ID.*
He goes behind the gauze to take the call –

Scene Four

ASSISTANT. Hi Arinzé, it's Rebecca from the agency, can I patch you through to your agent, is this a good time?

ARINZÉ. Well… not really, no –

ASSISTANT. Great, please hold.

ARINZÉ's put on hold for a beat. Then –

AGENT. 'Listen, you have just a little bit more attitude than I like.'

ARINZÉ. What? I don't have an attitude.

AGENT. 'Yes you do have an attitude. If you didn't have an attitude you would not raise your voice to me now would you?'

ARINZÉ. I'm not raising my voice, I'm engaging my diaphragm, *projecting* my voice because I'm at the theatre. Listen, I'm not gonna change the play –

AGENT. 'You don't seem to understand what I'm saying.'

ARINZÉ. Yeah I do, listen, if the producers think it's too political just because of the gentrification thing with the virus turning out to be blood cell then –

AGENT. 'This would not be the place to begin a career.'

ARINZÉ. – Firstly, it's not even that political. And even if it was, so what?
If the audience ain't ready to be challenged, maybe they shouldn't go to the theatre.

AGENT. 'People like going to theatres.'

ARINZÉ. I… I don't wanna discuss this with you, I'm gonna go.

AGENT. 'I'm the good guy – Do you understand? – I'm the good guy.'

ARINZÉ. If you were the good guy you'd be fighting my corner, you'd have my back on this one. I'm gonna worship Lucas's story, I think it's… the right thing to do.

PRODUCER. 'That's cos you're a baby and you don't know shit.'

ARINZÉ. Who is… is that… you're with him right now aren't you?

AGENT. 'Oh he's a handsome man – Got a good old head on his shoulders.'

PRODUCER. 'Your left nipple is a quarter inch higher than your right nipple.'

AGENT. 'You think so?'

PRODUCER. 'That's exactly the way I like it.'

AGENT. 'I'm really glad you're into this.'

Blast of porn noise.

ARINZÉ. Wow! Can you just, fucking, not do that in front of me.

AGENT. 'I made a mistake, I'm sorry, it will <u>never</u> happen again.'

ARINZÉ (*turns to* PRODUCER). Listen… I…

PRODUCER. 'What do you want from me? What the hell do you want?'

ARINZÉ. I just wanna get to the end with no one telling me how and what I should write. Is that too much to ask?

PRODUCER. 'You smoke crack don't ya?'

ARINZÉ. I… what?

PRODUCER. 'YA SMOKE CRACK DON'T YA?'

ARINZÉ. Crack cocaine?

PRODUCER. 'DON'T YOU SMOKE CRACK?'

AGENT. I… No. I don't smoke crack.

PRODUCER. 'It kills your brain cells.'

ARINZÉ. I just. I write. I just wanna write my shit unencumbered… and not even… I don't even *wanna* write the enlightening play that ticks all the boxes and bridges the racial and sexual and LGBT abyss, that some people expect of me. I just wanna write a play, man. A regular play. It's really not that deep. Everybody's just... the pressure, from both sides... can't this just fucking exist? Without it being a... an exotic... urban thing to someone, or a nigga play or without you thinking it ought to be unpolitical – what the fuck can you possibly know about what *I* wanna say? Can't it just be a play? Can a play from a person like me just be a fucking play already? Can we just hurry up and stop being weird about people like me writing plays and shit?

PRODUCER. 'You disappoint me brother, you disappoint me.'

ARINZÉ. It's just a story, about Lucas, about people like me, who don't want wanna get displaced by flat-white-sipping yoga addicts.

PRODUCER. 'I don't want you to blame the white man.'

ARINZÉ. No, I said 'flat white' not... I'm not blaming white people.

PRODUCER. 'Three of us will put our heads together and... I'm sure we'll be able to help you decide what's best for you to do – '

ARINZÉ. See that's exactly what I'm not trying to have us do, didn't you listen to *anything* I just said?

AGENT. 'It's gonna be a little different around here.'

ARINZÉ. I just wanna –

PRODUCER. 'This is not a damn democracy! – There's only one boss in this place and that's me!'

The call ends.

Scene Five

ARINZÉ *bounces his stress ball against the wall of the cube.*
This goes on for a while.
All of a sudden, every time the ball hits the wall of the cube,
there's a thundering bass.
ARINZÉ *throws the ball at the cube again but now, the ball has*
turned into a water balloon – we only know that when it bursts
against the cube.

There's sounds coming from within the cube.
ARINZÉ *goes to the cube and puts his ear to the wall, listening.*
ARINZÉ *begins to open the cube, he pulls the wall down until*
the interior of the cube is visible.

This whole scene is like a nightmare.
Inside the cube is ARINZÉ*'s study: desk, laptop, chair, lamp,*
etc., but everything is covered in orange and the room is filled
with balloons. It's as if his room is the interior of a balloon.
Sitting at the desk typing away is the little GIRL. *She swivels*
around in the chair and faces ARINZÉ. *When she talks, her*
voice is deep and demonic.

GIRL (*demonic voice, barely audible*). Oh, hey little bro!
    I didn't notice you there.
    I was just busy rewriting your play.
    (*Maniacal laugh.*)

    She hands ARINZÉ *a ghost balloon. Then she leaves*
    through the cube.
    ARINZÉ *goes in after her but she's disappeared.*
    Out of frustration ARINZÉ *starts bursting the balloons.*
    He bursts as many as he can.
    As he bursts the balloons a song begins to play (*not by the*
    MUSICIANS).
    Some of the balloons have an orange powder in them.
    ARINZÉ *becomes covered in orange powder. He removes*
    his shirt which is covered in the powder, so now the powder
    gets right on to his body. All over him. Bursting them
    becomes a dance. It represents the torment he's living with.
    It will go on for as long as necessary.

By the end of this, all the balloons are burst, ARINZÉ *is topless, exhuasted and covered in orange powder. However, even though there are none left, he's still bursting balloons. They're inside him now. They're inside his head. It's endless.*

Then there's a moment of surrender. A moment of acceptance. He gives in to them being there. He embraces them. He lets himself be influenced by them.

Scene Six

The BLOOD CELL *paces around topless... He gets rid of the mic-stand and paces with the mic on the wire. It's tense. It's like that moment an hour into a hip-hop concert where the artist is drenched in sweat, the stage is theirs. The audience is theirs. The length of the pauses between geh-geh's don't matter. There's conviction there. We've not seen the* BLOOD CELL *or* ARINZÉ *this bold before. When he begins performing, he gives everything, unashamed of who he really is, of his roots and of what people may think.*

'Geh-Geh'

BLOOD CELL
Geh-geh.
Geh-geh.
Geh-geh.
Geh-geh.

Geh-geh.
Geh-geh.
Geh-geh.
Geh-geh.

I'm at an arty virus cafe.
Geh-geh.
I told Tracy to meet me here.
Geh-geh.
I thought it was the old adventure playground.
Geh-geh.
Reached here to find out they've knocked it down.
Geh-geh.

And built this arty virus cafe.
Geh-geh.
I sit at a table, in the corner.
Geh-geh.
Dressed as this hipster, I've blended in.
Geh-geh.
Skinny virus waiter approaches me.
Geh-geh.

Is this, your only food menu?
Geh-geh.
So you don't even do a full English.
Geh-geh.
Yet you call yourself a cafe.
Geh-geh.
Ooh, 'Café' my bad.
Geh-geh.

Right. What is a croque madam?
Geh-geh.
So it's just egg, bread, cheese, ham.
Geh-geh.
And somehow costs eleven pound.
Geh-geh.
...wow.
Geh-geh.

I'll just, I'll geh-get a coffee.
Geh-geh.
You have a separate menu, for coffee.
Geh-geh.
Which one's, the normal coffee?
Geh-geh.
Just get me the one, everybody geh-gets.
Geh-geh.

Right, so, is this meant to be my coffee?
Geh-geh.
Why is it in such a tiny mug?
Geh-geh.
Why does the milk come separately?
Geh-geh.
I just like my milk inside my coffee, I'm crazy like that.
Geh-geh.

Know what, take it back, bring me a tea.
Geh-geh.
You can't have a separate menu for tea, bro.
Geh-geh.
You just, you can't.

Geh-geh.
No I do not wanna see the tea menu. No.
Geh-geh.

Get me a tea, just get it.
Geh-geh.
Just get it. A normal tea.
Geh-geh.
I know you have it. I know you do.
Geh-geh.
Get it if you wanna skateboard ever ageh.
Geh-geh.

Just want a tea and two slices of toast.
Geh-geh.
I'd like the milk inside my tea if that's okay.
Geh-geh.
White toast, buttered if that's okay.
Geh-geh.
Oh, and buttered, with butter, by the way.
Geh-geh.

I've been geh, like, geh-geh, and.
Geh-geh.
Think I'm infected geh, by geh geh, cos.
Geh-geh.
Ever since Jade geh, in the car, I've.
Geh-geh
I can't hold in, the geh, people are watching me,
Geh-geh!

Newspaper says police are still after me.
Geh-geh.
News is the man I beat died, of his injuries.
Geh-geh.
Now this hipster waiter has clearly noticed me.
Geh-geh.
He goes in the back, I geh-geh the fuck up and I leave.
Geh-geh!

I go to Tracy's school, pull her out of class.
Geh-geh.

We take the Tube, all the way to Regent's Park.
Geh-geh.
Get to London Zoo, Tracy joins the queue.
Geh-geh.
With a random school group, they let her through.
Geh-geh!

While the security guy was looking away,
Geh-geh.
I sneak through, the disabled-access gate,
Geh-geh.
But then he sees me at the last second,
Geh-geh.
He grabs his radio, I grab his neck and,
Geh-geh.

I tell him, to keep it stepping,
Geh-geh.
I take his radio and me and Tracy go,
Geh-geh.
Into the crowd, of people,
Geh-geh.
To find us now is like a haystack needle.
Geh-geh.

Tracy look! The kangaroo,
Geh-geh.
I told you we would go to the zoo, me and you,
Geh-geh.
You're the perfect height, you're very bright,
Geh-geh.
You can become any thing you like,
Geh-geh.

Taser! Taser! Taser!
Geh-geh.
Police tackle me down to the ground,
Geh-geh.
My shoulder pops out, I hear the sound,
Geh-geh.

Bones crack, knees on back, ow!
Geh-geh.

Struggling to breathe,
Geh-geh.
They're folding me like a long sleeve,
Geh-geh.
My ears pop,
Geh-geh.
Everything stops.

Everything does stop.
House lights come up.
ARINZÉ *pulls the plug out of the microphone.*
The band stopped playing immediately.

Scene Seven

The little GIRL *from earlier enters with the Dictaphone.*
She presses play on the Dictaphone.
We begin to hear ARINZÉ *and* LUCAS*'s interview continued.*
ARINZÉ *and the band continue packing away as this plays.*

LUCAS. ... and I'm just there kinda on my side now and my
    ears pop. I remember that, my ears pop.
    And sounds just went a bit different. Everything went
    different after that.
    Then I get this... everything goes, cloudy, but it's nice.
    And that's when I died.

ARINZÉ (*on Dictaphone*). Wow. That's... mad.

LUCAS. Tell me about it.

ARINZÉ (*on Dictaphone*). What was the last thing you saw?

LUCAS. Before I died?

ARINZÉ (*on Dictaphone*). Yeah, can you remember?

LUCAS. I was looking up. Last thing I saw... Yeah man. Yeah.
    I saw the balloon.
    Orange balloon floating away. Tracy was holding it before
    everything kicked off.
    Can't even remember how / she got it now.

ARINZÉ (*on Dictaphone*). / Fam you died! Fuck the balloon,
    you died!

LUCAS. Haha. I know man! When you die it's weird. It's like
    the sound of a choir.
    A choir of little girls. Sounds kinda sick. It's something to
    look forward to when you die.

ARINZÉ (*on Dictaphone*). So how are you even talking to me
    right now?

LUCAS. I don't know haha. You wrote this. You tell me.

ARINZÉ (*on Dictaphone*). I wrote this?

LUCAS. Yes.

ARINZÉ (*on Dictaphone*). So, I just made all this depressing
    shit up.

LUCAS. Haha. Yes.

ARINZÉ (*on Dictaphone*). WHY?

LUCAS. Haha I don't know. Ask yourself.

ARINZÉ (*on Dictaphone*). Arinzé, why man?

    ARINZÉ *stops what he's doing. A beat.*

    (*Live.*) I don't know.

LUCAS. You in the theatre now?

ARINZÉ (*resumes packing*). Yeah.

    (*On Dictaphone.*) They looking at you?

    (*Live.*) Yeah.

    (*On Dictaphone.*) This is awkward, man. You're a weird guy
    out here in these playwright streets. Seriously, why write this
    though urban safari jungle shit? You ain't thought about the
    responsibility and all that?

LUCAS. Arinzé don't care about no responsibility.

ARINZÉ (*on Dictaphone*). How you gonna end this jungle
    shit? –

    ARINZÉ *stops playback from the Dictaphone. He puts it*
    away.
    It's the end of the gig so they're packing away, winding up
    wires, turning off equipment, putting the drum sticks into the
    bag, the mics are zipped into their bags.
    STAGE MANAGEMENT *begin to clear the stage.*
    During this…

    ARINZÉ *or one of the two* MUSICIANS *pound their fists on*
    the desk or the floor.
    The others pick up on it and start chanting the words
    'Jungle Shit'.
    ARINZÉ *freestyling one last time, the* MUSICIANS
    back him with the 'Jungle Shit' chant after every line.

ARINZÉ *vibes to it, dances to it. He's free. Free from it all.*
He enjoys it more and more, becoming more tranced as it
goes on.

'Jungle Shit' (freestyle)

Jungle Shit,

Urban safari jungle shit?

Jungle Shit,

'Jungle shit', let's begin,

Jungle Shit,

Juh-juh-juh-juh-juh-juh,

Jungle Shit,

Apparently wrote jungle shit,

Jungle Shit,

Is that a sin?

Jungle Shit,

Is it for-bid-den?

Jungle Shit,

Firstly, define jungle shit,

Jungle Shit,

Our depiction on your TV screen?

Jungle Shit,

Radio, news, magazines?

Jungle Shit,

Is that what you mean?

Jungle Shit,

Lock your window and your door?

Jungle,

We're coming through the ceiling and the floor?

Jungle Shit,

Shithole country shit?

Jungle Shit,

An African? An animal?

Jungle,

An afric-animal? A cannibal?

Jungle,

Afric-animal cannibal satanical?

Jungle,

Primitive? Neanderthal?

Jungle Shit,

Jungle where we ought to be?

Jungle Shit,

Cracking nuts at the base of a tree?

Jungle Shit,

Banana eating?

Jungle Shit,

Chest beating?

Jungle Shit,

That what they mean by jungle shit?

Jungle Shit,

Does 'urban youth' come under it?

Jungle Shit,

I'm forbidden to write 'bout it?

Jungle Shit,

You hella protective over it,

Jungle Shit,

It's like it's some sacred shit,

Sacred Shit,

You mad that I lied?

Jungle Shit,

Does it even matter?

Jungle Shit,

That I told white lies,

Jungle,

White lies about black matters,

Jungle,

Don't you know black lies matter,

Jungle Shit,

If this shit was jungle shit,

Jungle Shit,

It won't be just any jungle shit,

Jungle Shit,

It be rainforest jungle shit,

Jungle Shit,

It be Jumanji jungle shit,

Jungle Shit,

Wakanda jungle shit,

Jungle Shit,

But this ain't jungle shit,

Jungle Shit,

This might be some Featre shit,

Featre Shit,

        With a capital 'F',

           Featre Shit,

    Cos where I'm from we say 'fanks man',

           Featre Shit,

      If they don't like my theatre shit,

           Featre Shit,

    They can suck my big black theatre dick.

Crash to BLACK.

End of Play.

A Nick Hern Book

Misty first published in Great Britain in 2018 as a paperback original by Nick Hern Books Limited, The Glasshouse, 49a Goldhawk Road, London W12 8QP, in association with the Bush Theatre, London

Cover image: Arinzé Kene by Bronwen Sharp

Designed and typeset by Nick Hern Books, London
Printed in the UK by Mimeo Ltd, Huntingdon, Cambridgeshire PE29 6XX

A CIP catalogue record for this book is available from the British Library

ISBN 978 1 84842 759 4

www.nickhernbooks.co.uk

facebook.com/nickhernbooks

twitter.com/nickhernbooks